A Glut of Avocados

Ann Carr

Illustrated by Martin MacKeown

MEREHURST PRESS
LONDON

The Publishers wish to thank
Rosemary Wilkinson and Malcolm Saunders
for their help with this book.

First published 1988 by Merehurst Press
5 Great James Street
London WC1N 3DA

Produced by
Malcolm Saunders Publishing Ltd
26 Ornan Road, London NW3 4QB

ISBN 1 85391 001 5

Photoset in Linotype Ehrhardt
by Fakenham Photosetting Limited
Printed in Spain

CONTENTS

Fuerte

FOREWORD

The cultivation of this pear-shaped fruit with its dark skin and pale flesh is relatively new. It is difficult to classify, as, botanically, it is considered a fruit but, since it is generally served as a savoury dish, it tends to be thought of as a vegetable.

Its firm, tough skin, sometimes crisp like bark, and its lack of scent or visible sign of inner texture have, I think, been two of the main reasons for the fact that it has taken so long to merchandise outside its native tropical and sub-tropical habitats. Other tropical fruit, such as the banana, have been on the market for so long we have forgotten whether they, too, had a struggle to become the very popular fruit they are now.

Like other tropical fruit, the avocado was perhaps first appreciated by the sailors who gratefully spread it on their dry ship's biscuits and called it 'midshipman's butter'.

The research for this book required that my family and friends consume a great many avocados but we never felt any benefit or side effect which could support their reputation as an aphrodisiac! Any racy reputation may

perhaps come from the name's derivation, for avocado comes from *ahuacatl*, an Aztec abbreviation for *ahuacacuahatl*, which was the name given to the tree and means 'testicle tree', probably because its fruit grows – and hangs down – in pairs. That the avocado was ever called 'alligator pear' was almost certainly nothing to do with any similarity between their skins. It was rather because the word 'ahuacatl' was an awkward mouthful and a similar-sounding name was applied. There are plenty of examples of this linguistic laziness: 'catsup' has nothing to do with cats but derives from 'ketchup', itself from the Malay 'kechap' or 'ketjap', the term for a sauce made from the juices of mushroom, walnut, tomato, etc. 'Plonk' is another example, to us it means cheap wine but in fact it is a corruption of the word 'blanc' from *vin blanc*, white wine.

Whatever the reasons for serving up your glut of avocados, you will certainly benefit from including them in your diet, for they are one of the most nourishing foods available. The recipes in this book are simple, practical, adaptable and, above all, show that the avocado is a fruit that is easy, economical and versatile to use.

The Nabal with its large stone

INTRODUCTION

It may seem unlikely that the avocado fruit and the spicy cinnamon bark could be related in any way but they are just two of the two-and-a-half thousand species of the *lauraceae* family. Two other well-known members are bay leaves, frequently used in cooking, and camphor, much used for coughs and colds and also in moth balls, as an insect repellent.

Avocados are the fruit *persea americana* of the family *lauraceae*; a tree native to the mainland of the western hemisphere from Mexico to the Andean regions. Avocados were widely cultivated as individual seedlings in tropical America before the Spanish conquest but were not cultivated intensively until horticulturalists found that the production of grafted trees was not complicated and gave the possibility of superior quality seedlings, which in turn would produce fruit of better quality and more uniform size and appearance. In about 1900 the first commercial avocado

orchards were cultivated and the fruit was subsequently developed in Florida, California and South Africa as well as, to a lesser extent, in Chile, Brazil, some of the islands of the Pacific and Australia. Large quantities are now grown in Israel and other countries round the Mediterranean and also in Kenya. It is curious that although these fruit would grow extremely well in the Orient, they are not generally appreciated or cultivated there. An acre of land will yield a large amount of food and could make a beneficial contribution in areas of poor diet and subsistence food production.

The avocado falls into three main groups: West Indian, Mexican and Guatamalan. The

Mexican avocado is small, weighing between 3 and 8 ounces (90 to 250 g), has a smooth, pliable skin and, for its size, a large stone. The West Indian is the giant and can grow as large as 2 to 3 lb (1 to 1.5 kg) in weight. It has a smooth, leathery skin and the lowest oil content. The Guatamalan is large, round in shape and weighs anything between 8 oz and 2 lb (250 g to 1 kg). Its skin is often warty and leathery and the avocado feels much less pliable when handled.

Avocado production in Australia, as in America, is a big, commercial crop. The main growing region is Queensland. Fuerte, Hass and Sharwil are the major varieties; others include Bacon, Edranol, Pinkerton and Anaheim. Some of these varieties come from California, (Anaheim is a suburb of Los

Angeles). Production is burgeoning to satisfy the demand for avocados in countries such as France and England at times of the year when northern hemisphere avocados are out of season.

Much folklore and myth are attached to the avocado and not without good reason for some of the myth is surely based on fact: the fruit is rich in vitamins and is indeed a fine food for a child-bearing mother to eat; its flesh is also rich in oils that soothe and heal and keep the skin supple, though, sadly, it is a fallacy that avocados will keep you eternally

youthful. Its reputation as an aphrodisiac comes not only from the testicle-like formation of the fruit on the tree but also from its high vitamin E content. This was certainly one of the vitamins recommended for infertility. In rice-growing economies rice, although it has no aphrodisiac properties, has for thousands of years been thrown at marriage feasts, fed to brides and given as a symbol of hope to young couples – because, like the avocado, it is rich in vitamin E.

And the avocado in the space age is still credited with magical powers, for it is said that man can live off avocados alone – and avocados are what the astronauts survive on in outer space! Whatever is claimed for it, the avocado is surely a food we should be using regularly in our diet, not as a treat, not as a luxury food, but as a food that is economical to buy, versatile to use and delicious and nutritious to eat. If it is true that 'an apple a day keeps the doctor away', why shouldn't 'an avocado a day keep illness at bay'?

Gluts of these beautiful green fruits do appear in our markets and are well worth taking advantage of. If you are lucky enough to buy a tray of unripe fruit, you can arrest the ripening process by keeping them in the vegetable drawer of the refrigerator. To ripen, leave in a warm, sunny spot or place in brown paper bags and ripen in the hot cupboard or near – not on – a warm radiator.

When choosing the perfect fruit to be eaten at once, do not squeeze the avocado, just hold it in the palm of the hand and gently increase the pressure: it should 'give' slightly if it is ready for eating. However, I find it preferable to buy the fruit under-ripe and to ripen it at home. This way it is less likely to be bruised.

Peeling a halved avocado

Peeling a whole avocado – always using a stainless steel knife

Cutting slices lengthwise
from a peeled avocado

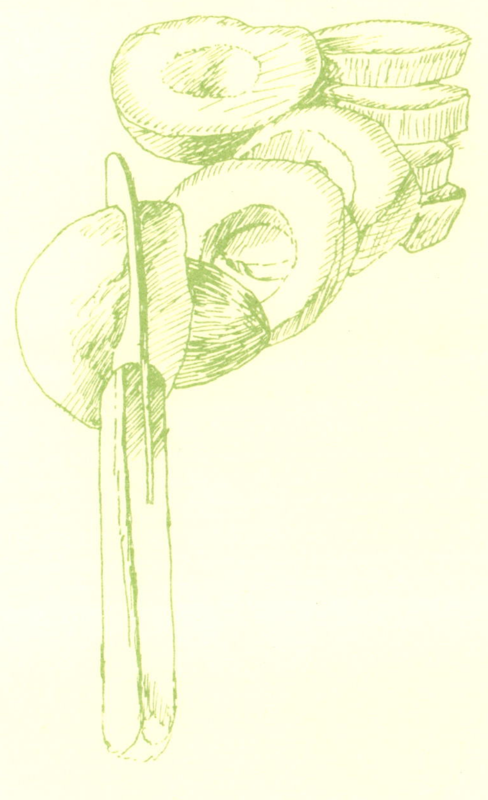

Cutting a peeled avocado in rings

Cubes of sliced avocado

Use a stainless steel fork to mash avocados

COOKS' NOTES

1. Unless specific details are given in the individual recipes, the following apply:
– spoon measurements are level
– sugar is granulated
– eggs are standard size
2. Follow either the imperial measurements or the metric but do not mix them, as they have been calculated separately.
3. As individual oven temperatures vary, use the timings in the recipes as a guide. Always preheat your oven or grill.

The Recipes

SAVOURY DISHES

The first essential is that your avocado is at the right stage of ripeness for the dish you are going to make. All too often one is offered the fruit when it is hard, crunchy and tasteless. The only use for slightly under-ripe avocados is in soups or sauces and even then they must be only just under-ripe. To use very ripe or over-ripe avocados for these, or any other dishes, generally means either that they discolour or that they are too acid for enjoyment because too much lemon has been added to prevent discoloration. Don't buy a bargain tray of over-ripe avocados and plan to feed the family on soups and mousses, it isn't worth it: those who don't much care for the fruit will be confirmed in their dislike and those who enjoy them in small doses will begin to suspect their judgement. There is, I'm afraid, a tendency to use the fruit in a far from perfect condition: a pity, for this is a delicious and versatile fruit, splendid in all sorts of usual and unusual dishes. It makes excellent soups, sauces, accompaniments to white fish and meat dishes, some desserts and also invalid food.

It is extremely good for the health, contains no cholesterol and is very easy to digest if in good condition.

As varieties of avocado do vary, if only slightly, in oiliness and texture, I find that the less oily fruits are best sliced or in salads, the buttery ones the most suitable for stuffing.

Both starters and main course dishes are included in this section since many of the recipes are interchangeable. Salads, for example, can be served as a starter or a side salad or made in larger quantities for a luncheon or supper dish.

As part of the diet for pregnant women, avocados not only contain folic acid, which is generally prescribed during pregnancy, but also are full of goodness and wonderfully easy to digest.

Avocados do not freeze.

Guacamole

It is appropriate to start this collection with what is perhaps the oldest avocado recipe. 'Guacamole' is Mexican and Mexico is the home of the avocado. There are many versions and variations of the recipe, for avocados are adaptable and their non-aggressive flavour lends itself to invention.

This is a good basic recipe with plenty of 'bite' to it.

Serves 4–6
2 large ripe avocados
1 tomato, skinned and seeded
1–2 teaspoons finely chopped onion
½ garlic clove, chopped
½ red pepper, seeded and chopped
1 green chilli, seeded and chopped
1 tablespoon lemon juice
salt and pepper, to taste

Peel avocados, remove stones and mash flesh, do not purée: this should be a dish of some texture. Add all other ingredients, mix well and serve with home-made brown bread, warm pitta bread, or any other well-flavoured bread. White, sliced loaf is not a suitable accompaniment.

Quick Avocado Soup

A basic recipe for a delicious, rich soup that is effortless to make. It can be served either hot or cold.

Serves 6

3 ripe avocados or 2 if very large

30 fl oz (940 ml) white stock

½ teaspoon Tabasco or other hot pepper sauce, or to taste

6 fl oz (185 ml) cream

6 fl oz (185 ml) plain yogurt

2 spring onions, chopped

2 tablespoons chopped fresh parsley

salt and pepper, to taste

Peel and stone avocados. Place flesh in a blender or food processor together with stock and Tabasco sauce. Process until smooth, then add cream and yogurt and whizz again. Add onions, parsley, salt and pepper and leave to chill for 30 minutes before serving.

To serve hot, heat very gently in a heavy-bottomed saucepan, on no account must it boil. Serve in very hot soup cups.

Abbogada pears (better known by the name of subaltern's butter).

(1829, Capt. Marryat 'F. Mildmay')

The mini avocado is much in demand: it looks like a small cucumber, about 3 in (7.5 cm) long, and has no pip. It is the result of unsuccessful flowering and is not, as often thought, a special variety.

Slimmer's sweet and sour avocado: mix together equal quantities of chopped avocado and chopped fresh dates, then toss with fresh orange juice, salt and freshly ground black pepper.

Avocado Soup Variations

The preceding recipe is excellent to use as a base for adding and subtracting flavourings. All these soup recipes are more likely to keep their clear pale colour if you use only unblemished fruit. In my experience, a lot of the problems with discoloration are due to the use of over-ripe or damaged avocados. One fruit with brown marks will discolour a whole batch of purée.

1. Add 2–3 skinned and chopped tomatoes as a garnish.

2. Substitute chopped coriander leaves for the parsley and add half a chopped green chilli, or more to taste.

3. Substitute 4 fl oz (125 ml) sherry for the yogurt and add 2–3 teaspoons of tomato purée or to taste.

4. Add juice and peel of 1 orange to the basic recipe.

5. Add 2 peeled, fresh, ripe pears to the basic recipe, processing them with the avocados.

6. Add half a chopped green pepper to the basic recipe, adding it with the onions, etc.

7. Add 1 very finely chopped red pepper and 2 peeled chopped tomatoes to the basic recipe but *do not* process them.

Avocado & Lettuce Soup

A lovely combination.

Serves 6–8

1 small onion

2 large or 4 small lettuces or lettuce thinnings

1½ oz (45 g) butter

good pinch mace

40 fl oz (1.25 litres) creamy milk

4 avocados

salt and pepper, to taste

Chop onion finely; wash, dry and roughly chop lettuces. Melt butter in a large saucepan, add onion and fry very gently for 10 minutes, do not allow to brown. Add lettuce and mace and stir-fry for 5 minutes, then add milk, bring to the boil and simmer for 5 minutes, taking care, for if the lettuce is at all bitter, boiling for too long or too fast will cause the mixture to curdle.

Peel avocados, halve, remove stones and purée flesh in a blender or food processor. Stir into the soup mixture, add salt and pepper, reheat gently and serve.

Slimmer's lunch: ½ avocado, chopped, mixed together with juice of ½ lemon, ½ teaspoon grated lemon peel, salt and plenty of freshly ground black pepper.

Prawn & Avocado Soup

A rich, luxurious taste, wonderful hot or cold and surprisingly easy to make.

Serves 8

1 lb (500 g) unpeeled fresh-cooked large prawns

1 oz (30 g) butter

8 fl oz (250 ml) dry white wine

4 avocados

40 fl oz (1.25 litres) creamy milk

salt and pepper, to taste

2 tablespoons chopped chives

6 fl oz (185 ml) double (heavy) cream

Shell prawns and reserve both shells and prawns. Melt butter in a large, heavy-bottomed saucepan with a tight-fitting lid, add prawn shells and stir-fry for 1 to 2 minutes, then add wine, cover tightly and

simmer for 5 to 10 minutes. Strain through a fine sieve or muslin and reserve. Pick over prawns and keep 2 or 3 of the biggest and best for each serving. Roughly chop remainder, place them in the saucepan and pour over wine. Peel avocados, halve and remove stones. Chop one of the avocados and add to prawns and wine. Purée remaining three.

To serve hot, stir in purée and slowly bring mixture almost to boiling point, stirring gently all the time. Before it boils, add milk, salt and pepper and reheat gently. Stir in chives, reserved prawns and cream, reheat gently again and serve.

To serve cold, remove from heat after adding purée and bringing almost to boiling point. Stir in milk, salt and pepper, cool, then chill. Just before serving, stir in chives, prawns and cream.

Avocado & Pear Soup

Serves 6–8

3 ripe avocados
4 ripe pears of good flavour
5 fl oz (155 ml) strong white stock
10 fl oz (315 ml) white wine
10 fl oz (315 ml) single (light) cream
1 teaspoon chopped spring onions
2 teaspoons soy sauce
1 tablespoon sesame seeds, to garnish

Place all ingredients except sesame seeds in a blender or food processor and purée. Serve this soup cold, garnished with sesame seeds.

Avocado Sweet & Sour

A delicious starter or light luncheon dish to serve with brown bread and butter, but remember that grapefruit 'kills' wine.

Serves 6

2 spring onions, chopped
1/2 clove garlic, chopped
1 tablespoon grainy mustard
4 fl oz (125 ml) honey
4 fl oz (125 ml) olive oil
2 fl oz (60 ml) wine vinegar
1 large firm grapefruit
4 large avocados
2 tablespoons chopped fresh parsley

Mix together onions, garlic, mustard, honey, olive oil and vinegar in a large bowl. Peel grapefruit, and, holding it over the bowl in order to catch the juice, remove all the white pith and carefully cut out the segments. Add segments to the mixture in the bowl. Toss gently and leave to marinate for 30 to 40 minutes.

Just before serving, prepare avocados. Peel, halve and remove stones, then slice each half into 6 to 8 sections lengthwise. Add to mixture, toss carefully, transfer to a serving dish and sprinkle with parsley.

Sweet Pickled Herring & Avocado

The sweet and sour fish complements the smooth avocado flesh.

Serves 8

2 herring fillets or rollmops

2 apples, peeled and cored

½ small onion, finely chopped

small piece pickled dill cucumber, finely chopped

2–4 fl oz (60–125 ml) sour cream

salt and freshly ground black pepper, to taste

4 avocados

black bread and butter, to serve

Chop fish and apples into roughly ¼ in (0.5 cm) cubes. Place in a bowl with onion and dill cucumber and stir in sour cream, salt and pepper. Halve avocados, remove stones and fill the cavities with the herring mixture. Serve with black bread and butter.

Israel has five main crop varieties, all of which came from Mexico via California. 'Ettinger' is the early cropper, followed by the two biggest croppers, 'Fuerte' and 'Hass'. The season tails off with the egg-shaped 'Nabal' and the almost-spherical 'Reed'.

Avocado with Carrots

This recipe uses the avocado as a vegetable. It is particularly good with poultry or pork.

Serves 4–6

1 lb (500 g) carrots

2 avocados

2 spring onions, chopped

½ in (1 cm) piece of fresh root ginger, grated

1 tablespoon chopped preserved or crystallized ginger

1–2 tablespoons white wine

1 oz (30 g) butter

salt and pepper, to taste

Scrape carrots and slice into rings. Steam or boil in salted water until just tender. Drain, then return to the pan. Peel, halve, stone and slice avocados. Add to pan with onions, both types of ginger, wine, butter, salt and pepper. Mix together very gently and heat through. Serve at once.

Avocado with Broccoli

Cook broccoli in the normal way, drain, then add 2 peeled, stoned and sliced avocados, 1 oz (30 g) butter, 2–3 fl oz (60–90 ml) double (heavy) cream and salt and pepper, to taste. Toss gently together and serve at once.

Hot Stuffed Avocado

This is a hot/cold starter – a surprise, with its cold shell and its hot stuffing. The secret is to have the avocados well chilled and to fill them quickly. Also, have the grill preheated.

Serves 4

Serve half an avocado per person

Fill with a stuffing made of:

4 tablespoons chopped cooked celery

4 tablespoons chopped cooked green beans

2 tablespoons chopped cooked carrots

1 tablespoon chopped spring onions

2 tomatoes, skinned and chopped

2 teaspoons sunflower seeds

2 teaspoons olive oil

salt and pepper, to taste

grated Gruyère cheese, to serve

Heat all stuffing ingredients, except cheese, together in a pan. Fill avocados and top with a good sprinkling of grated Gruyère cheese. Place under grill to brown.

There is a well-known West Indian fruit which we call an avocado or alligator-pear, and which the French call 'avocat' and the Spaniards 'aguacote'. All these names are corruptions of the Aztec name of the fruit 'ahuacatl'.

(1861, Tyler)

Avocado with Grapes

This is another hot/cold starter. Have the avocados and prepared grapes really well chilled before grilling, then cook quickly immediately before serving.

Allow half a medium avocado per person and 8 to 10 grapes, halved and seeded. An hour before serving, halve avocados, remove stones and brush with lemon juice. Fill the cavities with grapes and chill. Do not leave for longer than an hour, otherwise fruit may go brown. Just before serving, prepare sauce and heat grill.

Serves 4

½ oz (15 g) butter
1 oz (30 g) plain flour
4 fl oz (125 ml) milk
2–3 fl oz (60–90 ml) cream
1–2 fl oz (30–60 ml) dry sherry
dash of Tabasco sauce
salt and pepper, to taste
4 oz (125 g) grated Gruyère, Emmenthal or Swiss-type cheese

Melt butter in a small saucepan, stir in flour and cook for 1 minute over a gentle heat. Remove from the heat, add milk and stir continuously until smooth. Add cream and sherry, return to the heat and, stirring all the time, bring gently to the boil. Cook for 2 to 3 minutes, then add seasonings and cheese. Pour sauce over avocados and grapes. Grill under the preheated grill until sauce bubbles and begins to turn brown. Serve at once.

Note: There may be too much sauce but it is not practical to make a smaller quantity.

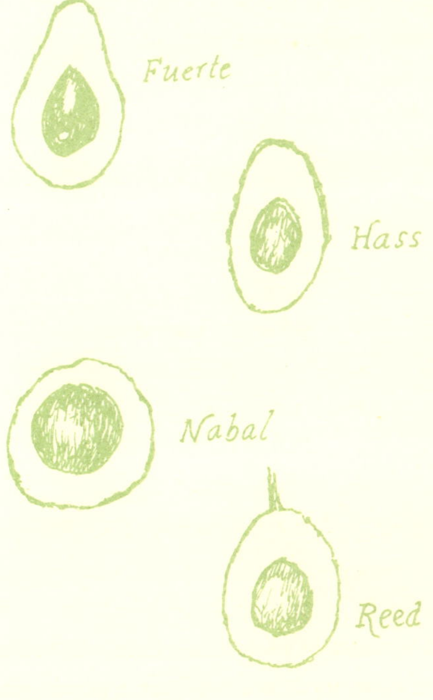

Halved avocados, showing the shapes and sizes of stones and flesh

Avocado & Lemon Sole Salad

Start this dish a day in advance. Allow 1 lemon sole per person and have the fishmonger fillet the fish for you, removing the black *and* the white skin.

This will serve 4 as a lunch or supper dish or 8 as a starter.

TO PREPARE THE FISH

4 lemon sole

10 fl oz (315 ml) fresh lemon juice

3–4 blades mace

6–8 black peppercorns, lightly crushed

SALAD

4 avocados

2 oranges

1 bunch watercress

1 tablespoon chopped chives

4 fl oz (125 ml) vinaigrette, made with 3 parts olive oil to 1 part vinegar

salt and pepper, to taste

Halve lemon sole fillets, making 4 pieces of fish per sole, lay them in a shallow dish, pour over lemon juice, then add mace and peppercorns, placing them carefully between the fillets to give flavour. Cover dish with plastic wrap and leave for 8 to 10 hours in the fridge, turning the fish and moving the flavourings around in the dish halfway through.

When ready to serve, peel, halve and stone avocados, then slice lengthwise. Peel oranges, remove all white pith and slice crosswise. Place avocado and orange slices in a salad bowl, add watercress and chives, pour over vinaigrette, sprinkle with salt and pepper, then toss together.

Remove fish from marinade, arrange fillets on a serving dish and place the salad round the fillets.

Godfrey's Avocado & Green Pepper Starter

Serves 4–5

4 avocados

1 green pepper

1 clove garlic, crushed

1–2 tablespoons lemon juice

4 tablespoons olive oil

salt and pepper, to taste

Halve avocados, remove stones and, using a dessert spoon, scoop out flesh. Transfer to a blender or food processor and whizz. Halve pepper, remove seeds and chop finely. Reserve a few pieces for decoration and transfer remainder to blender together with garlic, lemon juice, oil, salt and pepper. Whizz again briefly; the mixture should have texture. Spoon into glasses, decorate with reserved pepper and serve at once.

The West Indian varieties, for example 'Lula' and 'Booth', are round and smooth-skinned, juicy and not oily. They are grown in Martinique and Brazil and are considered by some to be the most flavoursome, but are not popular with the world market for this very lack of oiliness and butter-nutty flavour, which are now thought to be the proper characteristics of the avocado.

Avocado with Smoked Fish

Avocado and smoked salmon is a popular dish – delicious but unbelievably rich. Try this simpler version. Start a day in advance.

Serves 4

8 oz (250 g) smoked fish – halibut, haddock or cod will do

8 fl oz (250 ml) orange juice

4 fl oz (125 ml) lemon juice

2 spring onions, green and white parts

10 black peppercorns, crushed

1 tablespoon capers

6 fl oz (185 ml) sour cream

salt and pepper, if desired

2 medium avocados

orange or lemon peel, to garnish

Skin fish if necessary, place in a shallow dish and pour over orange and lemon juice. Chop white parts of spring onions and add to fish together with peppercorns. Cover with plastic wrap and leave in the fridge to marinate overnight or for 8 to 12 hours.

To serve, remove fish from marinade, dry and flake, do not make the pieces too small. Chop green parts of spring onions and capers finely into a small bowl. Mix together with sour cream, adding salt and pepper if necessary. Halve avocados, remove stones and fill the cavities with the fish mixture. Garnish with a slice of orange or lemon peel.

Avocado & Melon Vinaigrette

Serves 4

1 small melon

2 avocados

2 tablespoons chopped fresh mint

2 tablespoons chopped fresh parsley

1 tablespoon chopped chives

4 fl oz (125 ml) vinaigrette, made with 3 parts olive oil to 1 part vinegar

salt and pepper, to taste

Halve melon and avocados, remove seeds and stones and peel. Slice lengthwise and arrange in alternate, overlapping slices in a shallow serving dish. Mix herbs with vinaigrette, add salt and pepper and pour over fruit. Serve at once as a starter or a side salad.

Avocados with Orange & Mint Salad

Avocados are delicious with oranges. Allow a half of each fruit per person, peeled and sliced. Take care to remove all the white pith from the oranges. Add ½ tablespoon chopped fresh mint and 1 teaspoon chopped chives and toss in 1 tablespoon vinaigrette. Serve as a side salad with fish dishes or as a simple starter.

Avocado with Grapefruit & Onion

This combination makes a sharp, refreshing starter.

Serves 4

1 large grapefruit

1 small onion, finely chopped

1 teaspoon grainy mustard

2 fl oz (60 ml) vinaigrette, made with 3 parts olive oil to 1 part vinegar

2 avocados

Peel grapefruit, removing all white pith, and segment. Place in a bowl together with onion. Mix mustard with vinaigrette, then pour over grapefruit and onion. Chill.

To serve, halve avocados, remove stones and fill the cavities with the grapefruit and onion mixture.

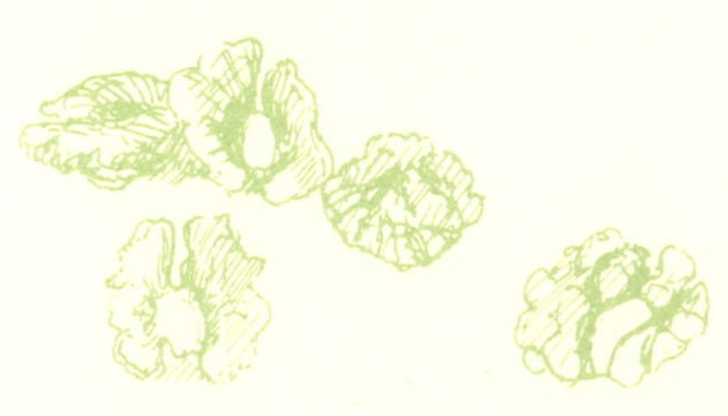

Avocado with Walnut Dressing

For each person you will need half an avocado, peeled and sliced, 3 or 4 walnut halves, chopped, 1–2 teaspoons currants, 1 teaspoon chopped fresh parsley and 1–2 teaspoons vinaigrette, preferably made with walnut oil. Toss all ingredients gently together and serve on a bed of lettuce leaves.

Although production is soaring, over 30% of the world's avocados are still grown in Mexico, where they have a twelve-month season because they are grown at different altitudes. Yet only a small fraction is exported, so the Mexicans must eat great quantities and be a healthy nation. They export 15,000 tons but consume over half a million tons!

Avocado & Carrot Salad

This is a wonderful mixture.

Serves 4

2 avocados

2 carrots

4 cardamom pods

3–4 fl oz (90–125 ml) vinaigrette, made with 3 parts olive oil to 1 part vinegar plus a few drops of garlic juice, *see page 60*

salt and freshly ground black pepper, to taste

Peel avocados, halve, remove stones and slice lengthwise. Peel carrots and grate on the coarse side of a grater. Place avocados and carrots in a salad bowl. Crush cardamom pods in a pestle and mortar, discard husks and add seeds to vinaigrette with salt and pepper. Pour over mixture in salad bowl and serve.

Avocado & Apple Salad

Another excellent combination.

Serves 4

2 avocados

2 firm apples, not too sweet

1 spring onion, chopped

4 fl oz (125 ml) vinaigrette, made with 3 parts olive oil to 1 part vinegar

salt and freshly ground black pepper, to taste

Peel avocados, halve, remove stones, slice lengthwise and place in a salad bowl. Wash and dry apples, do not peel. Grate on the coarse side of a grater, add to avocados together with spring onion, vinaigrette, salt and pepper. Toss gently and serve.

Avocado & Potato Salad

For this dish choose good firm avocados, preferably not too buttery in texture.

Serves 4

1 lb (500 g) new potatoes

2 firm avocados

2 spring onions, finely sliced

1 pickled dill cucumber, finely chopped

2 tablespoons chopped fresh dill weed

2 fl oz (60 ml) mayonnaise, preferably home-made

2 fl oz (60 ml) plain yogurt

salt and pepper, to taste

Wash potatoes and scrape if liked. Halve if large and cook in boiling, salted water until just tender, then drain, rinse under cold, running water, drain again and leave to cool.

When cold, cut into cubes ¼ to ½ in (0.5–1 cm) in size and place in a salad bowl. Peel and halve avocados, remove stones and chop to same size, then add to potatoes together with spring onions and dill cucumber. Toss gently. In a small bowl mix together dill weed, mayonnaise, yogurt, salt and pepper, then pour over the salad. Toss again and leave for 15 to 30 minutes before serving.

Note for slimmers: the avocado contains 33 Calories per 1 oz (30 g).

Avocado & Sorrel Salad

This is a perfect summer's day salad. The sharp sorrel leaves are wonderful with the creamy avocado.

For every avocado you will need a handful of young sorrel leaves. One avocado will serve 2 people. Peel and halve the avocado, remove stone and slice lengthwise. Wash and dry the sorrel and tear any large leaves by hand, then add to the avocado in a salad bowl.

VINAIGRETTE
2 fl oz (60 ml) orange juice
2 fl oz (60 ml) olive oil
1 teaspoon Swedish-style mustard
1/2 teaspoon grated orange peel
salt and freshly ground black pepper
few drops garlic juice, see method

Mix all ingredients together in a small bowl, then pour over the salad and serve at once. There may be a little too much sauce for two people but it will keep in the fridge.

Note: To obtain garlic juice, place a peeled clove of garlic in a garlic press, squeeze gently and slowly until the clove begins to ooze juice. Do not press hard or long enough to crush the garlic. Shake the drops into the vinaigrette.

Avocado & Egg Salad

You will need as many eggs as you have avocados. The eggs should be the smallest available.

Hard-boil the eggs, cool, peel and halve. Peel and halve the avocados, remove stones and paint all over with lemon juice or a mixture of vinegar and water in equal proportions. This helps prevent discolouring. Stuff each half avocado with half a hard-boiled egg and place in individual plates.

SAUCE (for 4–5)
1 teaspoon chopped onion
8 ripe tomatoes, skinned and roughly chopped
1 tablespoon chopped celery
1 tablespoon olive oil
2 teaspoons wine vinegar
salt and pepper, to taste

Place all ingredients in a blender or food processor and blend until smooth. Pour over and around the avocados and garnish with sprigs of fresh parsley.

Avocado & Bacon

This is an unusual main course, which is delicious served with pasta or floury boiled potatoes. It is important that the bacon is very thinly sliced, like Parma ham.

Serves 4

3 avocados

1 fl oz (30 ml) oil

8 oz (250 g) smoked back bacon, rind removed

1 teaspoon chopped spring onion

4–6 fl oz (125–185 ml) double (heavy) cream

1–2 fl oz (30–60 ml) plain yogurt

salt and freshly ground black pepper, to taste

Peel and halve avocados, remove stones and slice lengthwise. Heat oil in a heavy-bottomed frying pan and quickly flash-fry bacon. Remove, drain on absorbent kitchen paper and keep warm. In the same pan very quickly and carefully flash-fry avocado slices and onion, remove and keep warm. Add cream and yogurt to the juices in the pan, mix well and add salt and pepper. Arrange avocado and onion on a hot serving dish, pour over the sauce, add bacon and serve at once.

Do use a stainless steel knife to cut avocados.

Chicken with Avocado

Serves 4

$1\frac{1}{2}$ oz (45 g) butter

4 chicken breasts

1 teaspoon very finely chopped onion

2 tomatoes, skinned and chopped

1 avocado, peeled and chopped

2 tablespoons sherry

6 fl oz (185 ml) double (heavy) cream

salt and pepper, to taste

Slowly melt butter in a frying pan, add chicken breasts and fry gently for 4 to 5 minutes on each side, do not overcook. Remove from pan, cover and keep warm. Add chopped onion to the same pan and gently fry until cooked, then add tomatoes and fry for 2 to 3 minutes. Finally stir in avocado, sherry and cream, salt and pepper. Heat through, pour over chicken and serve.

Pot Roast Chicken with Avocado

This is a light and tasty dish with a lovely, simply-made sauce.

Serves 4–5

1 × 3 lb (1.5 kg) roasting chicken

1–2 fl oz (30–60 ml) cooking oil

8–12 cardamom pods, crushed

1 clove garlic, peeled

4 avocados

20 fl oz (625 ml) plain yogurt

salt and pepper, to taste

Wash chicken thoroughly inside. Reserve liver for another dish. Heat oil in a deep, flameproof casserole with a tight-fitting lid, add chicken and brown all over. Lower the heat, add cardamom seeds and whole clove of garlic, cover and leave to cook for 1 hour, turning on each side during cooking.

When bird is done, remove from casserole and keep warm. Strain off all fat and discard cardamom seeds and garlic. Peel 2 of the avocados, remove stones and purée flesh in a blender or food processor. Add purée to casserole together with yogurt and heat gently, stirring all the time, do not allow to boil. Peel remaining avocados, remove stones and chop, then add to the casserole. Heat through, add salt and pepper, then return chicken to the pot and serve.

As a vitamin source, the avocado is excellent. It contains such essential vitamins as A, B, B_2 and C, amongst others less familiar, such as E, K and HH.

As a mineral source the avocado is excellent for it contains many of the essential minerals: magnesium, copper, iron, calcium, phosphorus and potassium.

In parts of the world where avocados are indigenous, the fruit provide the main source of fats and oils in the diet, and so are a good meat substitute.

Avocado with Turkey & Sage

Sage is a strong herb but used carefully it blends well with the delicate avocado.

Serves 5–6

1 lb (500 g) boneless turkey breasts

2 oz (60 g) butter

2 avocados

4 sage leaves, finely chopped

6 fl oz (185 ml) double (heavy) cream

2 fl oz (60 ml) plain yogurt

salt and white pepper (freshly ground if possible), to taste

Slice turkey breast into thin escalopes (maybe your butcher will do this for you). Place slices between 2 sheets of greaseproof paper and very carefully and evenly beat out as thinly as possible. Gently heat butter in a large frying pan, add turkey escalopes and quickly fry on both sides. If they are really thin, they will not need more than ¾ to 1 minute each side. Remove to a hot serving plate and keep warm.

Peel and halve avocados, remove stones and slice lengthwise. Add to the pan with sage and gently heat through, then remove and keep warm with turkey. Add cream, yogurt, salt and pepper to the pan, stir together and heat through. Pour over turkey and avocado and serve.

AVOCADO SAUCES

Avocados make delicious sauces to accompany fish, white meats, vegetables and pasta. There are one or two important points to remember though. Avocados are rich, so if you are making a dish of pasta with avocado and cream, do have something light to start with or a fresh fruit dessert to follow. Also, if making a hot sauce, it is best cooked at the last minute to prevent discoloration. A cold sauce can accompany a hot dish and is often a delicious complement to it.

The recipes in this section are quick and simple to make and I have given examples of the kind of foods they would be best with.

Avocado & Dill Sauce

Use this with fish: try it with hot fried halibut or as an accompaniment to smoked trout or smoked salmon.

Serves 4

1 avocado, peeled, stoned and sliced
1 pickled dill cucumber, finely chopped
2 teaspoons chopped fresh dill weed
1 tablespoon plain yogurt
salt and pepper, to taste

Place all ingredients in a blender or food processor and whizz quickly: this sauce should have some texture.

The Avogato Pear-tree is as big as most Pear-trees ... the Fruit as big as a large Lemon.
(1697, Dampier 'Voyages')

Avocado & Walnut Sauce

Serves 4

1 avocado, peeled, stoned and chopped

1½ oz (45 g) walnuts

½ clove garlic

2–3 fl oz (60–90 ml) plain yogurt

salt and pepper, to taste

Place all ingredients in a blender or food processor and whizz. Serve with cold meats or gently heat through and serve with roast or grilled chicken.

The avocato, avocado, avigato, or as the English corruptly call it, Alligator-pear.

(1763, Grainger)

Avocado & Mustard Sauce

Good with ham or pork dishes.

Serves 4

1 avocado

½ oz (15 g) butter

6 fl oz (185 ml) single (light) cream

2 teaspoons Swedish-style mustard

1 teaspoon chopped chives or green tops of spring onions

salt and pepper, to taste

Peel and halve avocado, remove stone and chop into small pieces. Heat butter in a small saucepan, add avocado and stir-fry for 1 minute, then stir in cream, mustard, chives or spring onions, salt and pepper and gently heat through.

Avocado oil is used in fine soaps and is very soothing.

Avocado Sauce for Pasta

For this sauce use good, firm avocados – the best results are when the fruit has enough 'bite' to it to complement the texture of the pasta. The quantity here is enough for 12 oz (375 g) dried, uncooked pasta.

Serves 4–5

1 oz (30 g) butter

2–3 spring onions, green and white parts chopped

1 teaspoon grated orange peel

1 teaspoon grated lemon peel

½ teaspoon ground coriander, or to taste

6 fl oz (185 ml) single (light) cream

3 tablespoons plain yogurt

salt and freshly ground black pepper, to taste

2–3 avocados

Melt butter in a saucepan, add spring onions and stir-fry for 1 minute, then add orange and lemon peel and coriander. Remove from the heat while you prepare cream and yogurt.

Pour cream into a small bowl and add yogurt, salt and pepper, mix well until smooth. Peel, stone and chop avocados, add to ingredients in the pan, pour over yogurt mixture and very gently heat through; do not boil or avocados will become soggy and sauce will curdle. Pour over pasta, toss and serve at once.

Note: This sauce can be started in advance but the avocados should not be added until the last minute.

Avocado Sauce for Fillet Steak

This is delicious. If you have fried the steak, make the sauce in the same pan, using the lovely meat juices to flavour the sauce; otherwise use a small saucepan.

Serves 4–6

1 avocado

½ oz (15 g) butter

1 tablespoon Worcestershire sauce

8 fl oz (250 ml) double (heavy) cream

few drops garlic juice, see page 60

salt and pepper, to taste

Peel and halve avocado, remove stone and chop. Melt butter in a pan, add avocado and stir-fry for 1 minute. Stir in Worcestershire sauce, then add cream, garlic juice, salt and pepper, heat through and serve with the hot steaks.

Avocado & Ginger Relish

1 avocado, peeled, stoned and chopped

$\frac{1}{4}$–$\frac{1}{2}$ in (0.5–1 cm) piece of fresh ginger root, grated

1 teaspoon chopped spring onion

2 fl oz (60 ml) fresh orange juice

salt and pepper, to taste

Place all ingredients in a blender or food processor and whizz until smooth. Serve with hot fish dishes.

The fruit is called the Alligator Apple, but is not eaten as it contains a narcotic principle.

(1866, M T Masters, 'Treas. Bot.')

Filling slimmer's supper: 1 whole avocado, stone removed, filled with 2 tablespoons cottage cheese mixed with 1 teaspoon grated orange peel, 2 teaspoons chopped celery, salt and plenty of freshly ground black pepper.

Avocado & Lemon Sauce

Serves 4–5

1 avocado

1 teaspoon grated lemon peel

1 tablespoon lemon juice

6 fl oz (185 ml) single (light) cream

salt and pepper, to taste

Place all ingredients in a blender or food processor and whizz until smooth. Serve with hot or cold chicken dishes or with a delicate fish, such as sole or plaice.

SWEET AVOCADOS

Avocados are still a 'new food' despite their antiquity. This makes them very exciting to experiment with, for in fact, there is only a very short existing repertoire of recipes for them, most of which are for savoury dishes. The recipes given here form a short selection which I hope will encourage you to use avocados for desserts and investigate their use as a true fruit.

Avocados for dessert recipes must be firm, unbruised fruit, preferably of the juicy rather than the very buttery varieties. They will discolour easily, as the stocks or vinaigrettes or cooking in butter, which help prevent discoloration are used only for savoury dishes. So, do not attempt to prepare the dishes more than an hour or two in advance.

One avocado tree can yield up to 500 fruit.

Avocados with Rum & Brown Sugar

This is quick, simple and tasty.

Serves 4

3 avocados

2 tablespoons dark rum

3 oz (90 g) soft brown sugar

1 oz (30 g) butter, cut in cubes

Peel and halve avocados, remove stones and slice lengthwise. Pour rum into a shallow flameproof dish and carefully arrange avocado slices on top, making sure all are coated in a little rum. Sprinkle with sugar, dot with butter and place under a hot grill. Grill until sugar bubbles and begins to caramelise. Serve at once but take care when eating as the hot sugar topping can burn.

Avocado & Kiwi Fruit Salad

This is a favourite dish: cool, pretty and most refreshing.

Serves 2
2 kiwi fruit
1 avocado
2–3 cardamom pods
2–3 fl oz (60–90 ml) sugar syrup, see page 87

Peel kiwi fruit and slice in rings. Peel avocado, halve, remove stone and slice crosswise. Arrange both fruit in a pretty glass dish. Crush cardamom pods in a pestle and mortar, remove husks and sprinkle the roughly ground seeds over the fruit. Pour sugar syrup over fruit and leave for 30 to 40 minutes in a cool place. I think the wonderfully subtle and scented flavours of this dish are lost if it is refrigerated.

Avocado with Ginger & Orange

A very refreshing dessert.

Serves 3–4

2 avocados

2 oranges

½ teaspoon grated fresh ginger root, or to taste

1 tablespoon chopped preserved ginger

4 fl oz (125 ml) sugar syrup, see page 87

Peel and halve avocados, remove stones and slice lengthwise. Peel oranges, remove all white pith, slice into rings and arrange with avocados in a serving dish. Mix together the two gingers and sugar syrup in a small bowl, then pour over fruit and leave to marinate in the fridge for 30 minutes to 1 hour before serving.

Avocado with Mango Sauce

This is another revelation and shows how well these fruit, both still new to our tables, blend together.

Serves 3–4

3 ripe mangos

4 fl oz (125 ml) fresh orange juice

1–2 oz (30–60 g) caster sugar, or to taste

2 avocados

2 teaspoons chopped fresh mint, to decorate

To make mango sauce, peel mangoes, remove flesh and process to a purée together with orange juice and sugar in a blender or food processor.

Peel avocados, halve, remove stones and slice crosswise. Arrange in a serving dish, pour over mango and orange mixture and leave to marinate for 30 to 40 minutes, in the fridge if liked.

Just before serving, sprinkle with freshly chopped mint.

Israel's production of avocados is about 100,000 tons. US production is 150–200,000 tons. Australia's is 7,500 but expected to quadruple in a couple of years. Mexico's production is over 500,000 tons, 97% of which is home-consumed.

Avocado & Lime Fool

A pale green, cool fool in which the limes add 'bite'.

Serves 6
2 limes
3 avocados
2–3 oz (60–90 g) caster sugar
6 fl oz (185 ml) double (heavy) cream
6 fl oz (185 ml) plain Greek-style yogurt
a few green grapes, halved and seeded to decorate

Grate peel from limes and reserve, squeeze juice and reserve. Peel avocados, halve and remove stones. Purée flesh together with sugar in a blender or food processor, then

mix in grated peel and half the lime juice. Pour into a container just large enough to hold it and float remaining lime juice over the top. This should prevent too much discoloration and allow you to prepare in advance and assemble at the last minute. Cover with plastic wrap and refrigerate until needed but do not keep for longer than 2 hours. Whip cream, fold in yogurt, cover with plastic wrap and refrigerate until needed.

To assemble, pour avocado mixture into a bowl, stirring well to blend in lime juice. (Should there be any discoloration on the surface, remove with a teaspoon and discard.) Fold in cream and yogurt mixture, transfer to a serving dish and decorate with green grapes.

Avocado Custard

This dish is for those with an adventurous palate. It is both exotic and strange but do try it, for it is delicious. Use only just ripe fruit.

Serves 5–6

2 firm avocados

2 tablespoons rose water

4 egg yolks

1–2 oz (30–60 g) caster sugar

20 fl oz (625 ml) creamy milk

2–3 crushed macaroons

a few rose petals, fresh or crystallized, to decorate

mango sauce, see page 81, to serve

Peel and halve avocados, remove stones and slice lengthwise. Place in a shallow baking dish and pour over rose water. Place egg yolks in a bowl, add sugar and, using a wooden spoon, beat to the ribbon stage. Add milk and mix well. Carefully turn over avocado slices, pour over custard mixture, place in a bain marie and bake in a slow oven, at 150°–160°C (300°–325°F/Gas 2–3), for 1½ to 2 hours, or until custard is set.

When cooked, cool, then chill for 2 to 3 hours. To serve, sprinkle with crushed macaroons, decorate with rose petals and hand round mango sauce.

Most of Australia's varieties were brought from California in the 1940s but the 'Sharwil', unlike all the other main crop Australian avocados, was actually born in Australia from a chance seedling, in Queensland in 1951. The only other important Australian-born avocado is the 'Millicent', Queensland 1946, a light cropper and biennial.

Avocado Reviver

This is a slimmer's lunch, an excellent invalid diet or simply a pick-me-up.

In a blender or food processor place: 1 peeled, stoned and sliced avocado, the juice of 2 oranges, 3–4 tablespoons Greek-style plain yogurt, a pinch of ground ginger and a pinch of ground coriander. Whizz together.

To serve, pour into a bowl, sprinkle with chopped fresh mint and eat with a spoon.

To serve as a drink, add sparkling mineral water; as a reviver, dilute with champagne to taste.

Avocado cheers!

BASICS

Sugar Syrup

Yields approximately 20 fl oz (625 ml)

6 oz (185 g) sugar

15 fl oz (470 ml) water

Put sugar and water together in a heavy-bottomed saucepan. Heat gently until sugar has dissolved, then boil fast for 3 to 5 minutes. The syrup should have a creamy consistency and coat the back of a spoon. Leave to cool. Store in a screw-topped jar in the fridge.

Storing

Avocados do not freeze, they turn black and lose all texture and flavour. To store, buy unripe and keep in the vegetable compartment of the refrigerator for two to four weeks.

Never eat or cook unripe avocados.

Do not squeeze an avocado to test for ripeness: squeezing bruises the fruit, bruises discolour it and spoil its flavour.

The fruit of the avocado tree is, in fact, a berry and should be known as the avocado fruit, rather than the avocado pear.

The 'Horshim' is an Israeli hybrid, very similar to the 'Fuerte' but giving a later yield – November to March – and a good shelf life. It gets its name from a Kibbutz in central Israel.

INDEX

And thou green avocato, charm of sense,
Thy ripened marrow liberally bestow'st.
(1763, Grainger)